COUNTING BIRDS

To David Stemple, my father, who brought me on my first Count and whose legacy I continue every year as I get up at midnight to count owls. For the Hampshire Bird Club who compiles our count. For Steven Sauter and the Griffiths—Devin, Rae, and Aiden—who took over the Stemple territory. And for the OMG (my owling gang), who share my love of the "hunt," especially Susannah Richards, Lynn Pelland, Sloan Tomlinson, Brian Cassie, Stephen Swinburne, and Dennis Wehrly. —H. E. Y. S.

For Angus, my bird-loving brother. —C. R.

Thank you to Geoffrey S. LeBaron of the National Audubon Society, for his care in checking this work.

Brimming with creative inspiration, how-to projects, and useful information to enrich your everyday life, Quarto Knows is a favorite destination for those pursuing their interests and passions. Visit our site and dig deeper with our books into your area of interest: Quarto Creates, Quarto Cooks, Quarto Homes, Quarto Lives, Quarto Drives, Quarto Explores, Quarto Gifts, or Quarto Kids.

First published in 2018 by Seagrass Press, an imprint of The Quarto Group.
6 Orchard Road, Suite 100, Lake Forest, CA 92630, USA.
T (949) 380-7510 F (949) 380-7575 www.QuartoKnows.com

Seagrass Press titles are also available at discount for retail, wholesale, promotional, and bulk purchase. For details, contact the Special Sales Manager by email at specialsales@quarto.com or by mail at The Quarto Group, Attn: Special Sales Manager, 401 Second Avenue North, Suite 310, Minneapolis, MN 55401 USA.

Illustrations by Clover Robin

ISBN: 978-1-63322-604-3

Digital edition published in 2018
eISBN: 978-1-63322-605-0

Printed in China
10 9 8 7 6 5 4 3 2 1

COUNTING BIRDS

THE IDEA THAT HELPED SAVE OUR FEATHERED FRIENDS

BY HEIDI E.Y. STEMPLE
ILLUSTRATED BY CLOVER ROBIN

SEA GRASS

Frank Chapman loved birds.

He worked at the American Museum of Natural History in New York City creating exhibits about birds. He wrote books and magazine articles about birds. He studied birds' habits and habitats. He read the research of John James Audubon, the most famous ornithologist of all time.

Frank Chapman loved birds.

In 1899 he began his own magazine called *Bird-Lore*. Every two months, *Bird-Lore* was published and read by other bird lovers.

Around this time, Americans were
starting to think about the natural world
around them. First scientists and poets,
then government leaders, and finally more
and more regular citizens were starting to
talk about *conservation*.

How could they better live in their world?
How could they save the wilderness that was
disappearing, the forests that were being cut down,
the waterways that were being polluted, and the
animals and birds that were being overhunted?

But not everyone cared about conservation.

On Christmas Day, sports hunters would gather, choose teams, and hold a bird competition. All day long, the hunters looked for birds.

Large birds, small birds, all birds were game.

At the end of the day, the birds were counted.
The winning team was the side that had shot
and killed the most birds.

Frank Chapman did not love this tradition.
In the pages of his magazine, he set out to stop it.

Now Bird-Lore *proposes a new kind of Christmas side hunt, in the form of a Christmas bird-census, and we hope that all our readers who have the opportunity will aid us in making it a success by spending a portion of Christmas Day with the birds and sending a report of their 'hunt' to* Bird-Lore *before they retire that night.*

Count them, he proposed. But don't kill them.

That first year, on Christmas Day, 1900, 27 bird watchers, in 25 locations from Connecticut to California, counted common loons and killdeer, winter wrens and red-winged blackbirds.

BARRED OWL

FISH CROW

They observed hermit thrushes,
barred owls, Carolina chickadees,
fish crows, turkey vultures, and
spotted and canyon towhees.
In all, *Bird-Lore* proudly
reported close to 18,500
birds from 89 different
species.

Not one bird
was killed.

AMERICAN
GOLD FINCH

RED-WINGED BLACKBIRD

EASTERN BLUEBIRD

Purple Finch

Killdeer

Carolina Chickadee

Turkey Vulture

Winter Wren

Hermit Thrush

Common Loon

That first count was not the last. Every year, in December, more people join the count. Every year, more areas are added. And, every year, more and more birds are counted in every corner of the United States as well as Canada, Mexico, and Colombia. Other counts happen all over the world.

The owlers are the first ones into the field. They climb out of their warm beds at midnight and call down owls in the dark. By the light of the moon, they raise their hands to their mouths and whistle. They use recordings of real owls to hoot. They wait and listen. When an owl calls back, the owlers mark their maps and move on to the next spot.

When the sun starts to rise, so do fresh birders who arrive to take over. Some owlers say goodnight and some keep counting. All day long, groups observe and take notes in their count circles. Sandwich terns and song sparrows. Creepers, thrashers, bufflehead, brant, and bobwhites.

All birds are welcome.

Not all birdwatchers are in the field. Some count the birds that visit their backyard feeders.
All birders are welcome.

At the end of the day, the birders collect their notes and add their numbers. Later, the National Audubon Society will compile all the data and learn many things: how climate change affects bird populations, which species are in trouble, what areas need conservation help.

The birders know this is important for science, but that night, what is really important are their stories. Who found the most owls? Which rare birds were spotted? What records were broken?

The Audubon Christmas Bird Count has become the longest-running citizen science project and wildlife census in the world. Everyone wins. The birds. The birders. Science.

And all this because
Frank Chapman
loved birds.

More About Frank Chapman

Frank Michler Chapman (1864–1945) was a self-taught ornithologist. He was the associate Curator of Mammals and Birds before becoming the Curator of Birds in 1908 at the American Museum of Natural History. His magazine, *Bird-Lore*, eventually became *Audubon Magazine*, which is still published today.

In the modern Audubon Christmas Bird Count, each count area is a circle. A map point is identified and a circle with a diameter of 15 miles is drawn around it. This is the count circle. In November, birders sign up to participate in the count with local bird clubs and Audubon Societies. During one 24-hour period on a day between December 14 and January 5, each circle counts birds, compiles data, and reports to the National Audubon Society.

In 2016, which marked the 117th count, 73,153 birders (62,677 in the field and 10,476 at feeders) participated in 2,536 count circles. They counted 56,139,812 birds from 2,636 different species. Frank Chapman would be very happy with these results.

Would you like to count, too?

If you would like to be an Audubon Christmas Bird Count birder, contact your local bird club or Audubon chapter to find out if they participate in the Count. If they do, a good way to start is to join their feeder watchers. If you already have a birdfeeder, you can set up at a window to observe on a count day. But even if you don't have a feeder, you can watch for birds.

There are lots of great identification aids. I prefer a field guide book, but there are phone apps and computer sites that have tons of information, too. I use Audubon Owls on my smartphone, and I spend lots of time at the Cornell Lab of Ornithology website, www.allaboutbirds.org, which has identification, bird calls (including owl calls), and more.

For general information about the Count, visit www.audubon.org/ content/join-christmas- bird-count

FIND AN AUDUBON CHAPTER NEAR YOU:
www.audubon.org/ audubon-near-you

WANT TO GET INVOLVED IN OTHER WAYS?

There are many projects studying birds that are always looking for citizen scientists—young and old—to help collect data.

Each February, during President's Day weekend, participants in the Great Backyard Birdcount watch out their windows and report all their bird sightings online. This count, begun in 1998, is great for beginners because anyone can participate all day or even for just fifteen minutes (gbbc.birdcount.org).

To learn more about baby birds, scientists need the help of citizen scientists with a project called Nest Watch. To participate, citizen scientists sign up online and learn how to safely monitor nests. Then, once a nest is spotted, observation notes are recorded online (nestwatch.org).

There are more specific ongoing bird projects as well. Birds of all types, endangered and common, are being studied. Species, such as hummingbirds, hawks, kestrels, and condors, are being studied, and information is always welcomed by groups like the Journey North, Hawk Watch International, American Kestrel Partnership, and Condor Watch.

HUMMINGBIRD

KESTREL

CONDOR

A note from the author

Many kids first learn about owling from the 1988 Caldecott Medal–winning book, *Owl Moon*, by author Jane Yolen, who happens to be my mother. *Owl Moon* is a family story. I am the little girl in the book. My dad, David Stemple, took all of us—both my younger brothers and me—out into the woods by our home in western Massachusetts to call down owls. He taught us to call and to listen. When I moved back home after living in the South for many years, I started joining him on the Audubon Christmas Bird Count. After his death, I continue to owl the count with his map and his recordings. I learned from the best. And I am pretty good.

GREAT HORNED OWL

BARRED OWL

EASTERN SCREECH OWL

I don't call owls often, except in schools where I talk to students about writing, but, once a year, I am one of the Audubon Christmas Bird Count owlers I talk about in this book. I go to bed around 7:00 PM and set an alarm for midnight. I climb out of my warm bed and lead a team of owlers for seven and a half hours calling and counting owls. We call ourselves the OMG—the Owl Moon Gang. On our best night, in 2012, we called down 67 owls— 54 Eastern Screech Owls, 9 Great Horned Owls, and 4 Barred Owls. When I reported my numbers at the gathering where our data was collected, everyone *oohed* and *aahed*. There is still a bit of competition, after all. But no birds are harmed. Thanks to Frank Chapman.